7.00
+H

41 - 3353

3 - 15 - 63

THE WALTER LYNWOOD FLEMING

LECTURES IN SOUTHERN HISTORY

LOUISIANA STATE UNIVERSITY

1940

THREE VIRGINIA FRONTIERS

THOMAS PERKINS ABERNETHY

RICHMOND ALUMNI PROFESSOR OF HISTORY
THE UNIVERSITY OF VIRGINIA

Gloucester, Mass.
PETER SMITH
1962

To

ANNIE PIERCE ABERNETHY

MY MOTHER

FOREWORD

The Walter Lynwood Fleming Lectures in Southern History, sponsored by the Graduate School and the Department of History of Louisiana State University, were inaugurated in 1937 to honor a former professor of history who distinguished himself as a scholar, researcher, and writer in the Civil War and Reconstruction periods.

Professor Fleming was a native of the South and a graduate of Alabama Polytechnic Institute and Columbia University. He taught at West Virginia University in his early years and completed his professional career at Vanderbilt University. In the interim, some of his most productive years were spent at Louisiana State University, 1907–1917. In all, some ten books and one hundred and sixty-six articles and reviews came from his pen. As a historian, his name stands for impartial yet sympathetic investigation of an important epoch in southern history.

The inaugural series of lectures, "Behind the

Lines of the Southern Confederacy," was given by Professor Charles W. Ramsdell of the University of Texas, April 14–16, 1937. The second series, "The Repressible Conflict, 1830–1861," was delivered by Professor Avery Craven of the University of Chicago, February 21–23, 1938. "Conditioning Factors in Southern Agriculture in the Ante-Bellum Period," was discussed in a third series given by Herbert A. Kellar, Director of the McCormick Historical Association, Chicago, March 7–9, 1939. The fourth series, here printed, by Professor Thomas Perkins Abernethy of the University of Virginia, was delivered February 27–29, 1940.

AUTHOR'S PREFACE

The Walter Lynwood Fleming lectures, delivered by the author at Louisiana State University in February, 1940, are here presented without material alteration. They do not purport, in any sense, to constitute a history of the Virginia frontier. Because the tidewater, the piedmont, and the transmontane regions of the Old Dominion appear to be fairly representative of the first three stages in the development of the American frontier, they are treated as illustrative examples of the general theme. In tracing their development, the author has been impressed with the manner in which the democratizing influence of the frontier was largely offset by such countervailing factors as European customs and traditions, British legal systems, and the methods by which the public lands were disposed of. These forces must be given their proper place in the picture before a balanced delineation of frontier conditions can be attained. No more than a mere suggestion of this problem is herein attempted.

Any effort at scientific discussion is handicapped by the loose manner in which the terms "west" and "frontier" have commonly been used by historians who have stretched the frontier thesis to make it cover practically all the democratic movements which have taken shape in this country. One illustration of this is the way in which the liberal ideas of Thomas Jefferson have often been accounted for on the basis of his middle class origin and the frontier conditions under which he grew up. Unfortunately, neither the origin of his ideas, his background, nor his environment has been understood by this school of writers. In this case, as in many others, the reasoning has been of the a priori variety.

Perhaps an even better example of how hazardous it is to deal too categorically with the "west" is furnished by Georgia in the years following the War of 1812. At that time Georgia's piedmont section was the "west" but the most exposed frontier was the southeast. The former section controlled the government of the state and, by adopting a general ticket for the election of congressmen, at times deprived the east of representation. This situation tends to prove that much that has commonly been lauded as western democracy was merely western self-interest and was not a particularly significant factor in the building of a "government of the people, by the people, for the people."

Of the invaluable work being done at Louisiana State University in promoting the study of the history of the South, the author is keenly appreciative; and for the opportunity to have some small part in honoring the memory of a sympathetic friend of early years and one of the South's great scholars, he is grateful.

Thomas Perkins Abernethy

University of Virginia
April, 1940

CONTENTS

[xiii]

I

TIDEWATER

PERHAPS the principal problem confronting the historian is this: Does history consist of a never-ending series of connected events which he may describe and even sometimes explain, but the underlying causes of which are so complex that he can never hope satisfactorily to account for them? or are there certain fundamental factors which influence all history and make it possible to integrate the story of the progress of the human race? In other words, is the writing of history an art or is it a science?

The fascination of the frontier thesis as applied to American history lies in the fact that it stresses a basic factor which has significantly influenced the development of our national habits and institutions and makes it possible to account for them, at least in part, in a scientific manner. But the frontier influence is only one of many factors which have played a part in our national development, and for proper interpretation it should be considered from a proper perspective. First of all, America was settled by Europeans who brought with them their European institutions and traditions. Having separated themselves by a broad ocean from the source of their culture, the early colonists were brought face to face with an environment of which they knew practically nothing; and so poorly qualified were they to cope with it that it took them more than a hundred years to push the frontier from Jamestown to the Blue Ridge Mountains.

In order, therefore, to understand the significance of the frontier in American history, it is essential to begin by considering its impact upon those who were first to face it. Moreover, in its progressive development we must keep constantly in mind the two conflicting forces which were at work: that is, the leveling tendency of the frontier on the one hand, and the European traditions and customs of a stratified society on the other.

Frontier conditions were not always the same. We must take into account not only the existence of boundless tracts of virgin land, but the legal system that governed their settlement, the pecu-

liarities of the people who colonized them, and the
economic conditions under which migrations took
place. It will not be safe to generalize about the
significance of the frontier in American history
until there are available to us detailed studies of
the various areas involved, and only a start has
been made in that direction.

Toward this end, therefore, it is the object of
these discussions to trace the development of the
conflict between European institutions and frontier conditions in one specified area—Virginia, our
first frontier—as her boundaries existed at the
time of the Confederation, with the Atlantic
Ocean as her eastern limit and the Mississippi
River as her western.

Within these borders we have four fairly distinct divisions to consider: the tidewater, the piedmont, the valley, and trans-Appalachia which included the territory now constituting the states of
West Virginia and Kentucky. Here we have a
variety of conditions which present the frontier
in such contrasting circumstances as to cast its
essential characteristics in bold relief. Yet until
1792 the entire area was always subject to the
same, though a changing, system of law; and consequently the frontier never had an opportunity

[3]

for complete self-expression. It is, however, just such limitations upon frontier development that must ever be taken into account before a satisfactory knowledge of the subject may be attained.

The pioneer John Martin, who stepped from the *Susan Constant,* 100 tons burthen, to the sands of Jamestown in 1607, was markedly different from the pioneer Daniel Boone, who traveled the Wilderness Trace to the Kentucky country in 1775. Many factors of a peculiar nature influenced the development of society among the English colonists who first reached the shores of North America. Unlike later pioneers, these first adventurers were not capable of furnishing their own means of transportation. This was a selective factor in determining the types of persons who made the voyage, and it had an important bearing upon the conditions under which they settled.

Among other things, it obviously resulted in the establishment of three economic levels among the inhabitants of the southern colonies. In the case of Virginia, those who could pay not only for their own transportation but also for that of others were granted land in proportion to the number of persons whose passage they paid. Such men became the large landowners, the gentlemen who could live by the sweat of other men's brows, the dominant class in the colony. Those who could finance the migration only of their own families were likewise granted lands in proportion to their numbers. They became the yeomen who tilled their own soil and voted for members of the House of Burgesses. Their ranks were augmented as the indentured servants achieved freedom and acquired lands, but this was not altogether easy to accomplish and the middle class was never as powerful or as self-assertive in Virginia as it was in the northern colonies where servants were less numerous.

These servants were, in the main, the people whose expenses of migration were paid by others. In order to liquidate the debt they became indentured to planters as agricultural laborers, usually for terms of five years. Those brought over by the London Company were given small tracts of land at the expiration of their terms of service and thus at once rose into the ranks of the yeomen; but after the dissolution of the company, no such grants were made to the freedmen until 1705. During that interval they could acquire farms only by purchase or by securing headrights; that is, in effect, paying for the transportation of other colonists. This cost about six pounds per person and was beyond the means of most freedmen. For this reason many of them migrated to regions where the land laws were not enforced, notably to the neighborhood of Albemarle Sound and the Roanoke River in North Carolina.

Thus the situation in regard to transportation and landownership resulted in the development of a marked stratification among the early settlers and served to counteract any leveling tendency that frontier conditions are generally supposed to produce. And there were still other factors which reinforced this tendency.

One of these was the slowness with which the early settler, who cautiously hugged the coast for decade after decade, adjusted himself to frontier conditions. Later pioneers learned to build for themselves substantial cabins out of the logs which they readily obtained from the forest. But if the seventeenth century American desired anything better than the crudest sort of hut, he knew how to build only a brick or timbered house such as he had known in England; and, with all the timbers and clapboards to be hewn and split by hand, this was a major undertaking, to be accomplished only by the more industrious and prosperous minority.

So it was with all those essential crafts that characterized our later frontiers. Wheat did not thrive in virgin soil but the Indians taught the colonists to grow corn, and this was their first major adjustment to the new environment. Yet they still found it difficult to procure adequate food. Though the waters teemed with fish and the forest with game, they had no experience as fishermen and their clumsy firearms did not produce the results of the frontier rifle of the eighteenth century. Consequently, during the first years food often had to be brought from England or obtained from the natives. This was especially hard on the poorer people who depended for their subsistence on the labor of their hands. And how was the average newcomer to make soap or candles, to grow flax and spin and weave his clothing? Perhaps, after the growing of corn and tobacco, the pioneer's next major achievement was to learn from natives the art of making moccasins and clothing from deerskins and other peltry and to dress himself somewhat in the Indian fashion. We know little of the beginnings of this custom, and the wealthier families of the seaboard never adopted it; but it was a godsend to the poor, though in some degree a badge of their poverty.

As a result of all these circumstances, it was necessary for the early colonists to import from England many things that later pioneers made for themselves. Therefore, living on any but the lowest possible economic level was quite expensive and tended to emphasize class distinctions. Conditions were much improved when the culture of tobacco was introduced. Then, even the poorest settler might have something with which to procure from abroad the articles necessary to his existence. Later frontiersmen carried on little trade with the outside world and consequently developed social conditions peculiar to themselves; but in tidewater Virginia navigable water was everywhere accessible, and the universal demand for imported articles made it necessary and practicable for nearly everyone to grow a little tobacco in order to purchase a few commodities brought from Europe. Thus the whole population was kept to some degree in touch with a far-flung commerce. More than a century after the founding of Jamestown, the Reverend Hugh Jones wrote that "the Virginia *Planters,* and even the *Native Negroes* generally talk good *English* without *Idiom* or *Tone,*" and that it was hardly to be distinguished from the speech of London "which they esteem their

Home." It was the English of Shakespeare's time which the pioneers brought to Jamestown, for the Bard of Avon was not to die until nine years after the little band of sea-weary men landed in Virginia. However, relatively few of them came from the metropolis on the Thames, and the speech of London in the seventeenth century was less like that of the rest of England than it is today. But Virginia traded extensively with London, and her people gradually discarded the peculiar speech of their native provinces and adopted that of the merchants and sea-faring men. Thus we are furnished with a good illustration of the manner in which oversea commerce affected the life and customs of the tidewater region.

This commerce brought the mother country home to nearly every colonist and kept alive in the New World the customs and traditions of the Old. Among these was the recognition of social stratification. The poverty-stricken colonist of Jamestown did not compare himself with his prosperous neighbor and forthwith rebel at the thralldom of class just because he had arrived on a "frontier." He accepted his status because he had never known anything else.

In addition to the economic forces that tended to

breed and maintain class distinctions, there were legal and governmental factors that worked in the same direction. England had long maintained a stratified society and in many ways, both directly and indirectly, her laws as well as her social customs recognized and enforced this condition. Though Virginia acquired her own legislative body in 1619, it was stipulated that all colonial legislation should conform as nearly as possible to that of England; and during the earlier part of the seventeenth century it was commonly admitted that Parliamentary statutes were generally applicable in the colonies even though the acts themselves made no special provision to that effect. During the eighteenth century the common doctrine in Virginia was that statutes passed before 1607 had general application in the colony but those passed since that time applied only in case they carried a clause specifically extending them to the dominions. In addition to this, the common law of England was, of course, applied by Virginia courts so far as they understood it.

This undemocratic body of law and precedent was reinforced by many undemocratic acts of the colonial government itself. Until the latter part of the seventeenth century, the members of the governor's Council were exempt from taxation; and only they, according to an early statute, could wear gold braid upon their clothes. They were appointed to many of the lucrative offices within the gift of the governor and the Crown; and since the governor and the Council controlled the public lands, they were often in position to further their own ambitions to accumulate great estates. The Council, made up from the wealthier landowners, certainly constituted a colonial aristocracy; and since, once in office, their tenure was much more secure than that of the governor, most of whose acts required their approval, they were naturally favored in many ways by the local representative of the Crown.

Not only was the administration of the colony aristocratic but so was that of the several counties. The justices of the peace, who controlled both the judicial and executive business of the counties, were appointed by the governor; and the vestrymen, who controlled affairs of the established church, after their original election by the parishioners filled their own vacancies. Other officials, such as the county surveyor, the county lieutenant, the sheriff, the coroner, and the clerk, were also appointed; and the people were left with absolutely no voice in the administration of local affairs or the levying of local taxes.

As would be expected in these circumstances, taxes fell most heavily upon the poor. By far the greater part of the cost of government was met by the imposition of a poll tax. This was divided into three categories: the public, the county, and the parish levies. In each case the expenses of the jurisdiction were estimated and the amount arrived at was divided by the number of taxable polls. This gave the amount to be assessed against each. All male inhabitants over sixteen years of age, whether bond or free, and all female servants and slaves of that age were counted as polls or tithables. Thus, a poor man with a family of five tithables would pay half as much in poll taxes as would his rich neighbor with a family of the same size and five slaves or servants over sixteen years of age. Taxes on real and personal property would have tended to equalize this burden, but there were few such levies before the latter years of the eighteenth century and even then they were mostly of a temporary nature. Prior to that time there were usually no land taxes as such, but a quitrent of two shillings the hundred acres was levied on all estates. If this may be regarded as a tax, it was certainly a modest one; and since the same rate was charged for all land regardless of quality, the tax fell more heavily upon the poor than upon the rich. The only other taxes of any importance were export duties on such articles as peltry and tobacco, and import duties on liquors and slaves, but these last were often disallowed by the Crown after brief periods of enforcement. Yet these were minor items in the budget and did not materially affect the general picture of taxation per capita and per acre rather than taxation according to ability to pay.

In addition to these political and economic factors, there were others of a less obvious nature tending to emphasize social stratification. The importance of the family as the fundamental social unit has long been recognized. On the other hand, the tendency of the frontier to develop individualism is one of the best known of modern historical concepts. But the conflict between the stress on family and the glorification of the individual has usually escaped notice in this connection.

The English tradition as well as British law strongly favored the concept of the family. The institutions of primogeniture and entail aptly illustrate this tendency. But there are other more obscure examples. The custom of chaperonage, the difficulty of obtaining divorce, the right of the husband to control the actions and property of his wife and to make the important decisions for his children, all illustrate the weight attached to the solidarity of the family and the small concern for individual rights.

Nothing was done in seventeenth century Virginia to weaken the legal bulwarks by which the unity of the family was maintained, and since the laws of the colony had to conform to those of the home country, it is not certain that much could have been done. But it is not probable that there was any desire to change the situation. A social system founded upon the soil does not change rapidly, and relative isolation upon the farm where all interests are shared in common tends to maintain cohesion in the group. The father strives to acquire property so that he may provide marriage portions for his children and leave them an estate when he passes on. Thus the family is a continuing entity that ties the past to the future and perpetuates tradition.

In any rural society where stratification is the rule, family pride counts for much, and an individual rarely passes altogether on his own merits, but on the status of the family to which he belongs. This is not so absurd as it may seem, for where family feeling is strong the individual must view his actions as they affect the group. For instance, in choosing a wife a young man must consider not only his own feelings toward the woman of his choice; since she must be closely associated with his family and he with hers, the approval of both connections is essential. In many ways this restraint has a salutary effect. Relatively high standards of conduct and manners are likely to be maintained, and this is especially apt to be true of a rural aristocracy. On the other hand, such a situation makes it difficult for one to rise above his origin.

Though colonial law furnished no indication that European conceptions of the family were being broken down, it cannot be denied that frontier conditions were likely to make their first inroads upon established institutions at this point. Where land was plentiful and cheap, it was not necessary for a father to provide so carefully for the future of his children, and consequently their feeling of dependence upon him was proportionately weakened. Many young men and women, especially among the lower classes, often undertook to fend for themselves. Thus individualism began making headway against family cohesion and when, during the period of the Revolution, Americans began to shape their own institutions, this change was reflected in the law. But in this case, as in all others, it took the frontier a long time to do its work.

Another peculiarity of a rural aristocracy, such as that of seventeenth century Virginia, is that while class consciousness is strong, class conflicts do not readily develop. One reason for this was well-established custom. The Englishmen who came to America had never known anything but a stratified society and they accepted subordination as a matter of course. The fact that in Virginia class distinctions were implicit in the organization of both church and state tended to prevent any change in the social structure. Furthermore, in a rural community where each family had its own system of subordination and where there were few towns to offer a rendezvous for the more restless spirits, there was scant opportunity for the dissemination of equalitarian ideas.

The local influence of the justice of the peace and the vestryman also bolstered the position of the aristocracy. Since the people elected none of their county officials, they were commonly chosen from among the more opulent planters. Their opportunities for oppression and exploitation were enormous and as neither justice nor vestryman received any remuneration, it would not be surprising to find them seeking compensation in indirect ways. That they did this cannot be denied. The county surveyor selected choice tracts of land for himself, and the justice used his influence to get himself elected to the House of Burgesses; but there were no professional politicians in seventeenth century Virginia and the tradition of public service was well established. Though it is difficult for a world grown bourgeois and proletarian to admit it, the agrarian did not think of life altogether in economic terms. Public honor often counted more than private gain, and public sentiment in a rural community where every man knew his neighbor would not have tolerated the tricks that were commonly practiced in cities by merchants and tradesmen. In all societies dominated by a rural aristocracy there is a tendency for the planter to despise the trading class. This is partly due to a clashing of economic interests, but it is affected by conflicting standards of economic morality. There can be no question that in the staple-producing areas the colonial period engendered in the local squirearchy a spirit of public service which bore rich fruit during the period of the Revolution and which, since the advent of the professional politician, has suffered a steady decline.

Another reason for the lack of social conflict was the absence of obvious economic competition between the classes. It is true that the rich reaped nearly all the rewards and the poor bore nearly all the burdens of life in the staple colonies. Though the opulent planter preëmpted the best lands and worked them with the labor of indentured servants and slaves, nevertheless the yeomen farmers who elected the Burgesses and constituted the backbone of society felt themselves quite independent of the aristocracy. Since their votes were essential, they were cultivated by the local magnates, and the price of tobacco did not depend on the social standing of its producer. The presence of Negroes produced a certain solidarity among the whites, and custom demanded courtesy and good manners in all dealings between man and man, regardless of class. This, it is true, involved a certain deference from the lowly toward the more exalted, but where class distinctions are of ancient vintage they are not commonly resented. It might be added that they are never entirely absent in any society and that their justification depends upon the public worth of the dominant class.

Thus we find in early Virginia a firmly entrenched social stratification, one which was established by law, supported by custom, and accepted without serious question by all classes. For a hundred years frontier conditions made only minor inroads against it.

But democracy may exist even where social stratification is recognized. If England can claim to be a democracy, this must certainly be true. Do we find, then, in seventeenth century Virginia any definite trend toward liberalism in government; if so, was it more or less than in the mother country, and was it due in any degree to frontier influence?

With the establishment of the House of Burgesses, Virginia began her political career under liberal auspices. All freemen were allowed to vote for members, whereas in England a forty-shilling freehold was the qualification in the shires for voting for members of Parliament. One reason for this liberalism was doubtless the fact that the "planters" in Virginia were as much members of the London Company as were the "adventurers" in England who held stock, and there was no reason why the latter group should undertake permanently to rule the former. The liberal views of Sir Edwin Sandys were also a telling factor in all major decisions made by the company at this time. While the associates in London had the right to veto acts of the colonial Assembly, the reciprocal privilege of vetoing acts of the company was promised to the Assembly. Furthermore, the charters of the organization provided that settlers in Virginia should have the same rights as though they were still resident "in our Kingdom of England." Therefore, during the latter years of company rule, the Virginians appeared to enjoy a greater degree of political freedom than did their brethren who remained at home. In the other southern colonies it was on the religious rather than the political side that greater freedom was enjoyed, for they offered toleration in order to attract settlers. In Virginia the Anglican church was established from the beginning, and none but Anglicans were supposed to reside in the colony prior to the Toleration Act of 1689. It should not be inferred from this, however, that none others came.

When the London Company was dissolved in 1624 and James I, with his dislike of representative bodies, became the lord and master of Virginia, the future looked dark for liberalism in America and in Virginia, now become the first royal colony. Meetings of the House of Burgesses lapsed for several years, but when it reassembled under royal authority its constitution was not appreciably changed: all freemen were still allowed to vote for members, whose powers remained much the same as under the company. What these powers were was never made entirely clear during the colonial period, and the War of the Revolution was finally fought over this issue as it affected Virginia and her Continental sisters.

While admitting that Parliamentary legislation had effect in the colonies, during the seventeenth century the Burgesses repeatedly claimed the sole right to pass local legislation and impose local taxation in Virginia. There were occasions when the governors tried to raise money without their consent, but they always resisted and royal officials were never able to establish any such right. Near the end of the century, the Virginians, at the cost of their own immediate welfare, even opposed and temporarily prevented the establishment of a postal system on the ground that the postage would amount to a tax levied without their consent.

The question arises as to whether a struggle for

local self-government is a struggle for democracy. Since the local government may be quite as undemocratic as the one which seeks to control it, there is reason for denial that the question of democracy is necessarily involved here; yet the House of Burgesses was a more democratic body than was Parliament, and it more nearly represented the interests of the people of Virginia than Parliament possibly could. Thus the struggle for self-government in this case at least was certainly a struggle for democracy since that term involves the idea that the people should have some voice in the enactment of legislation. As stated, a certain degree of democracy is not incompatible with the existence of aristocratic institutions. In fact, the two ordinarily do exist side by side in varying degree.

Though Virginia thus commenced her career with extensive privileges of self-government and a suffrage as broad as any known in America until recent years, time and the frontier did not work in favor of democracy in the Old Dominion during the seventeenth century. The first important change, however, was in that direction. During the Commonwealth period Virginia was in effect a self-governing colony, enjoying free trade with the rest of the world and prospering because, free from British maritime restrictions and duties, she was getting high prices for her tobacco. But when the Stuarts were restored, Virginia welcomed Sir William Berkeley back to his former post as governor, and the old political system again went into force.

Yet it was not for long that the loyal subjects of the Old Dominion had reason to rejoice. Once more all Virginia's tobacco had to be sold in England, and the Navigation Acts of 1660–63 bore heavily upon her commerce. Poverty was widespread among the planters. Governor Berkeley, by the judicious use of official patronage, allied himself with the members of the colonial Council and for more than a decade refused to hold the customary annual election for Burgesses. Thus the people were deprived of any voice in the government of the colony and were impoverished by British restrictions on their trade. It was under these circumstances that an Indian invasion set off the only serious rebellion that colonial Virginia ever experienced.

Whether this affair, known as Bacon's Rebellion, was a manifestation of frontier democracy has been a controversial question. Since it developed out of an Indian incursion, the frontier was naturally the first section affected, and most of the colonial magnates rallied to the Governor's support. But Bacon himself, only two years from England and a member of the Governor's Council, was hardly a typical frontiersman; nor can his leading supporters be classified in that category. Social lines were not strictly drawn in the contest, nor was the line between east and west. It was a rebellion against a governor who usurped the established rights of the people. It differed from the greater revolt of a hundred years later mainly in that it was aimed primarily against Berkeley rather than against the British Crown, and in that the Governor had been able to ally a considerable part of the aristocracy with his cause. But in view of the fact that England herself had recently experienced political disturbances of an even more serious nature, it is hard to see that Bacon's Rebellion represents any special demonstration of frontier democracy. It represents rather, just as does the Puritan Revolution in England, the desire of the people to safeguard rights to which they considered themselves entitled under the constitution and established by ancient custom.

The reactionary regime against which Bacon re-

belled is illustrated by the fact that in 1670 a freehold qualification was required for the suffrage
which had previously been enjoyed by all freemen.
Bacon undertook to restore the old system, but
when his rebellion was put down Berkeley re-
established the freehold qualification and it was
not again changed during the colonial period. This
was only the beginning of reaction. The defeat of
Bacon gave Berkeley his opportunity, and the governors who followed during the seventeenth century carried on the movement which was in line
with the illiberal policy of the British Crown during the latter years of the Stuart period.

The annual elections and regular sessions of the
House of Burgesses were not restored, the governor now having the right to adjourn, prorogue,
and convene the Assembly as he saw fit. In 1680
the governor and Council began to sit separately
from the House, and this body lost its appellate
jurisdiction over cases coming up from the General
Court. The governor had formerly communicated
his instructions to the Assembly, but he was now or-
dered to do so only when the home government
authorized such action. It was in 1680 also that the
Burgesses granted in perpetuity to the Crown a
two-shilling export tax upon each hogshead of to-

bacco, thus making the governor's salary independent of popular control. The same period saw the establishment of vice-admiralty courts in the colony, thereby making it possible to try without a jury anyone committing an offense against the customs and navigation acts; and in 1692 slaves were for the first time tried without juries. Other reactionary moves to levy taxes without consent of the Burgesses and to deprive them of their right to initiate legislation were defeated. Thus a century which started with a very liberal regime in Virginia ended in a wave of reaction. This change was brought about, not by local conditions but by policies formulated overseas, and therefore it has no direct bearing upon the question of frontier democracy. It simply goes to show that new country, which normally offers certain opportunities to the underprivileged, will not necessarily breed democracy unless it has a chance to control its own destiny; and this opportunity has rarely been present in the history of frontier development.

Of course, in other phases than the political there are ways in which the frontier may shape society along more liberal lines than those to which it has been accustomed. But it has been shown that social stratification, supported by law and custom, was maintained in tidewater Virginia despite frontier conditions, and on the economic side there was a sharp demarcation between rich and poor. The establishment of distant colonies is necessarily a highly capitalistic venture; and experience proved that, so far as the southern plantations were concerned, no adequate return on the investment was to be expected without the establishment of relatively large-scale agricultural operations involving the employment of indentured servants and slaves. The failure of Oglethorpe's philanthropic experiment in Georgia would seem to prove this point.

The conclusion must therefore be that the frontier should offer something more than the forest if it is to produce democracy. It must offer cheap or free lands which are easily accessible to the penniless immigrant, which was not the case in early Virginia. It must offer a system of agriculture which makes subsistence farming possible, and its people must know something of the crafts and skills necessary to frontier existence. In other words, it must have a population which by long experience has adjusted itself to frontier conditions. None of these factors was present in the seventeenth century, and the results were such as might have been expected.

In any phase of life it takes a people a long time to develop institutions that are congenial to its circumstances and environment. If many generations passed in America before a typical native literature was written or typical American music composed, it should not be surprising that more than a century elapsed before political and social institutions began to take on the color of the American scene. During the eighteenth century some beginning was made in that direction, and our next object will be to trace this development in the piedmont area and the Valley of Virginia.

II

PIEDMONT AND THE VALLEY

THE turn of the eighteenth century brought many changes to Virginia. Some of them were caused by purely local circumstances; others grew out of events occurring across the Atlantic. Of fundamental importance among the latter was the Glorious Revolution of 1688. When James II was driven from England and William of Orange by Parliamentary action seated upon the throne, a long struggle had reached its appointed end. Henceforth there could be no question that Lords and Commons, rather than the King, were the real rulers of Albion's Isle, and it was natural, in the course of events, that they should undertake also to extend their jurisdiction to the dominions over the seas. In fact, their general legislation had long been recognized there, but the Burgesses and Council had from the first claimed the right to pass all local laws and levy all local taxes. Royal governors had attempted without success to infringe upon these customary privileges. Parliament was one day to try it and to shatter the empire in the attempt.

But the changed complexion in England had more immediate effects upon the colonial scene. Formerly the enclosure of lands for the purpose of raising sheep had turned many laborers off the soil and produced an army of unemployed. Many of these found their way to the staple colonies as indentured servants, and it was thus that the earlier planters had recruited their labor supply. Now England was developing by handicraft methods the manufacture of her own wool, and the unemployed were finding work. Consequently there were fewer laborers seeking the American shore; but the organization of the Royal African Company in 1672 tended to supply this deficiency and to substitute black for white labor in Virginia, where the number of slaves had been quite small prior to the last decades of the seventeenth century. Despite many disadvantages, slave labor proved to be economically profitable and the larger planters came to depend more and more upon it.

Though white servitude did not disappear from the colonies during the eighteenth century, the

origin of the servants changed. The place of the
English laborer of the seventeenth century was
now taken not only by the slave but by Protestants
from the north of Ireland, along with other Scottish and Irish people and by Germans from the
Palatinate and neighboring provinces, together
with some German-speaking Swiss. The illiberal
economic policies which William III enforced in
Ireland and the devastation caused on the Con-
tinent by the wars following his accession were re-
sponsible for the migration of these peoples. Another policy of William's reign facilitated their
naturalization in Virginia; for the Toleration Act
of 1689 made it, for the first time, legally possible
for dissenters to carry on public worship according
to their own tenets though it was still necessary for
them to pay tithes for the support of the established church.

By the year of William's accession, settlement
in Virginia had reached the falls of the James
River. In 1679 William Byrd I had acquired large
tracts in that neighborhood, but the progress of
colonization was slow and it was not until half a
century later that his son established the town of
Richmond at that point. The James was the most
natural route to the West in Virginia, but it was

only during the second decade of the eighteenth century that settlement began to extend above the falls. Meanwhile, a queer deflection of the westward movement had been brought about by Governor Alexander Spotswood, who administered the colony from 1710 until 1722.

In addition to the James there were two other rivers which could be followed by those seeking western lands and homes. These were the Roanoke and the Rappahannock. The former was inferior to the other two for purposes of settlement because it emptied into North Carolina's Albemarle Sound where there was no really good port for the shipment of tobacco. The Rappahannock did not lack shipping facilities, but its course, lying to the north of the James, was not so near to the center of population. It was this stream however which Spotswood undertook to develop as the first avenue to the West, and it is a reasonable assumption that he did so because Byrd had preëmpted the strategic commercial position at the falls of the James.

Spotswood was a military man, and when he first arrived in Virginia he began to pay special attention to the frontiers. The local Indians were no longer a menace and a profitable trade was carried on with them by William Byrd and others. Philip Ludwell was also interested in this trade and barter, and he and his relatives, the Blairs and the Grimeses, dominated the Governor's Council. The principal center of the Indian trade was Occaneechee Island, located at the point where the Staunton and the Dan join to form the Roanoke River. Here the rebel Bacon had once defeated the assembled savages in a fierce battle, and here several Indian paths converged. One of them, formerly used by the Dutch to carry on a trade with the Virginia Indians, came down by an eastern route from New York through Pennsylvania. Another, called the Great Warrior's Path, came down the Shenandoah Valley and crossed eastward over the Blue Ridge where the Staunton River cuts through the mountains. The Iroquois from New York used this route to make forays against the weaker Indian tribes in Virginia. Another path led southwestward to the Cherokee villages on the upper waters of the Tennessee River.

In the days before Bacon defeated the Occaneechee and their allies, a Virginia trader by the name of Abraham Wood, with headquarters at Fort Henry where Petersburg now stands, carried on trade with Indians at the island, who in turn got furs and skins from the Cherokee and other western tribes. Anxious to know more about the sources of supply, Wood sent out explorers and in 1671 his agents, Thomas Batts and Robert Fallam, reached the New River. They were thus probably the first Englishmen to look upon the waters of the Mississippi basin. Returning to their outpost, they triumphantly reported that they had seen "sayles" on the South Sea. But these explorations were not followed up, and when Spotswood reached Virginia little was known of the western mountains or the rivers which flowed beyond them.

The French had been more active. In 1699 they established a settlement at Biloxi on the Gulf, and in 1702 Mobile was founded. In the former year they made a settlement at Cahokia in the Illinois country and another at Kaskaskia the following year. Detroit was founded in 1701. Now the problem of Spotswood, the soldier, was to maintain peaceful relations with local tribes, to protect them from the Tuscarora and the Iroquois, and to extend the Virginia frontier across the mountains so as to cut off the French settlements on the St. Lawrence from those on the Gulf. He wished also to develop the Indian trade and to regulate the granting of public lands in order to promote settlement and to bring more revenue into the royal coffers. If in doing all these things he could increase the weight of his private purse, his enthusiasm for the public service would be in no way diminished.

No sooner had he reached the province in 1710 than he sent out explorers, who reported within the year that they had climbed the steep slopes of the Blue Ridge. At about the same time the Governor reported that iron mines had been discovered near the falls of the James, and proposed to the British Board of Trade that special inducements be offered to settlers who would migrate up this river and establish themselves on its banks. He even envisaged the planting of settlements as far as the Great Lakes, which he thought lay at a short distance beyond the mountains, hoping thus to disrupt French communications on the western waters.

But the Governor soon lost interest in the James River as a route to the West. It was not long after the beginning of his administration before he found himself at loggerheads with the Ludwell-Byrd faction which controlled his Council. Their interest in the trade of the James and Roanoke rivers has been mentioned. It thus became necessary for Spotswood to strike out along different lines. In 1712 he organized a group of promoters, and soon

the discovery of deposits of iron near the falls of
the Rappahannock was announced. The next year
he induced the Burgesses to permit him to establish
a fort on each of the three main rivers and to colo-
nize the tributary Indians at these points.

It is needless to say that no post was erected on
the James, but in 1714 Fort Christiana was built
on the Meherrin, a tributary of the Roanoke, the
Saponi Indians were settled near it, and an Indian
school established. But civilizing and Christianiz-
ing the natives was not the Governor's chief objec-
tive. In December of the same year he prevailed
upon the Assembly to charter the Virginia Indian
Company which he had organized, and to give it a
monopoly of the Indian trade south of the James.
Headquarters were established at Fort Christiana,
and the Governor had reason to think that he was
making headway against the faction of the Byrds
and Ludwells.

Yet it was the Rappahannock area that claimed
his main attention. The Tuscarora, who had been
driven out of North Carolina, were to have settled
here, but they went to New York and joined the
Iroquois to constitute the sixth tribe of the northern confederacy. It was actually a very different

people who formed the colony on the Rappahannock.

Shortly after the year 1700 the canton of Berne, Switzerland, sent two agents, Christopher de Graffenreid and Ludwig Michel, to America to find an asylum in Pennsylvania, Virginia, or the Carolinas for some of her war-ridden people. In 1706 Michel visited the Conestoga section of Pennsylvania, and within three years Palatine Germans and Swiss emigrants began to settle in that region. It was in 1706 also that de Graffenreid agreed to purchase ten thousand acres in North Carolina. Though he never paid for the lands, as a result of this transaction he was dubbed a landgrave by the provincial proprietors.

The Scottish Earl of Orkney and several prominent Englishmen were interested in Spotswood's ambitious colonizing and iron mining schemes, and through them the Governor arranged with de Graffenreid that some of his German and Swiss miners should be sent to Virginia. The first contingent arrived in 1714 and they were settled near the iron ore deposits on the Rappahannock. The colony was christened Germanna, and the Governor persuaded the Assembly to build a church, a road, and a fort for the benefit of his project. Since the British authorities had refused to sanction any move looking toward the development of iron works in Virginia, Spotswood kept the real purpose of his venture secret, but the miners were, by public authority, enlisted as rangers for the protection of the frontier.

Of course these German immigrants were granted no land, but were given the status of tenants on large tracts which Spotswood took up in the neighborhood. Becoming dissatisfied with their lot, many of them left the employ of the Governor and established settlements of their own higher up the country near the mountains.

Most of the German and Swiss refugees, as is well known, made their way not to Virginia but to Pennsylvania, where they settled in Chester, Lancaster, and other counties east of the mountains. By 1717 they were joined by large numbers of Presbyterians from the north of Ireland, as well as by other Irish and Scottish elements. Most of these people came as indentured servants, but when their terms of service expired, they found lands in Pennsylvania too expensive and some of them were settled by Lord Fairfax on his holdings between the Rappahannock and the Potomac. There is evidence that there were a few living on the Potomac as early as 1719.

South of the Rappahannock, where the lands belonged to the royal domain, Virginia was now in position to offer a more attractive haven to men seeking homes in the New World. Whereas in the seventeenth century it was necessary to pay about six pounds for the transportation of an immigrant in order to obtain a "headright" claim to fifty acres of land, since 1699 it had been possible to purchase headrights for five shillings each. In other words, the price of land had dropped from twelve pounds to ten shillings the hundred acres. But in addition to paying the headrights, one had to "improve" his land and pay annual quitrents amounting to two shillings the hundred acres. Improvement meant the building of a cabin and clearing at least one acre for every tract granted. In 1705 Parliament had offered a bounty for the production of naval stores, and this had encouraged men to survey large tracts and exploit their pine forests without ever going through the formality of securing a patent, thus avoiding the necessity of paying the quitrents and making the necessary improvements. In order to remedy this situation, Spotswood was instructed to enforce a more stringent system of regulations for the granting of lands. His first move was to issue a proclamation declaring that anyone wishing to acquire more than four hundred acres should obtain an order from the governor and Council rather than merely from the county court. Furthermore, in 1713 he secured the passage of an act providing that all landowners, regardless of how long they had held titles to their tracts, should be required to cultivate three acres out of every fifty of arable land. This would tend to prevent the taking up of large tracts by men who had no intention of settling upon them.

Then, coming back to his scheme of frontier settlement, he secured the passage in 1720 of an act creating the two new counties of Spotsylvania and Brunswick. The former included his Germanna lands and was to extend westward so as to take in the pass over the Blue Ridge which he, with the convivial "Knights of the Golden Horseshoe," had penetrated in 1716. Brunswick County lay along the North Carolina boundary and was to include the water gap where the Staunton River breaks through the Blue Ridge. Thus the passes through the mountains were to be occupied in order to prevent any eastward incursions of the French, and the Governor's interest in frontier lands was to be promoted. The Burgesses exempted the settlers in these new counties from taxation for ten years, and the home government was petitioned to exempt grantees from the payment of headrights and quitrents for the same period.

In order to take advantage of these anticipated benefits, the Governor and a group of his friends secured orders from the Council to take up immense tracts in the new county of Spotsylvania; but the home government, after some delay, limited exemption from headrights and quitrents to tracts of one thousand acres or less, and the speculators failed to reap the full reward of their astuteness. Nevertheless, the new county was developed by Spotswood and his associates and by 1727 settlements had been extended westward as far as the foot of the Blue Ridge Mountains. In 1728 the first land grant was made in the valley of the Shenandoah to men who had crossed the mountains from Spotsylvania.

Thus the cautious advance of approximately two hundred miles from Jamestown to the Valley had required nearly one hundred and twenty-five years. This period had bred a new race which in the next one hundred and twenty-five years, with superb mastery of its environment, pushed the frontier from the Valley of Virginia to the last outpost on the Pacific.

Because of its unpromising commercial situation, Brunswick County was not settled for some years, and the next westward advance took its course up the valley of the James. Lacking official support or special concessions but occupying the most accessible river valley in the upcountry, this movement is of particular interest. Starting from the falls, settlement did not extend much above them until the decade of the 1720's. Then, within a period of ten years, the central piedmont was occupied by its first settlers and landowners. Here, as in the Rappahannock region, it was not the ex-indentured servant seeking a home in the backwoods who first appeared. On the contrary, the trail was broken by a group of prosperous men who needed new lands for the cultivation of tobacco, for the establishment of their younger sons on plantations of their own, and for purposes of speculation.

The leadership in this movement up the James was taken, not by the Byrd family with its large tracts about the falls, but by the Randolphs. The patriarch of this important colonial family, William Randolph, had settled in 1684 on Turkey Island Creek near where Governor Dale had built the town of Henrico in 1611. Nearly opposite this point the Appomattox flows into the James, and in the neighborhood were settled many prominent seventeenth century families, including such well-known names as Carter, Eppes, Branch, and Bland. Near here also at "Mount Malady" resided Thomas Jefferson, grandfather of Peter, and great-grandfather of Thomas, the President. Just upstream from Turkey Island the James makes a broad sweep and forms a peninsula known as Curles Neck. Here one of William Randolph's sons, Richard, who married Jane Bolling, built his home; while another, Thomas, passed above the falls and established his seat at Tuckahoe, which is reputed to have been the first estate developed on the upper James. He acquired the tract in 1710, but, like most of the early purchasers, developed it for some years before taking up his residence there. Still farther up the river, just above where Goochland Court House was later located, a third Randolph brother, Isham, made his home at "Dungeness"; and near by, Tarleton Fleming, who married a sister of the Randolphs, built "Rock Castle." In the same neighborhood settled the Bollings, descendants of John Rolfe and Pocahontas. Not far away on Bremo Creek, the Cockes, kinsmen of the prominent Cary family, established themselves. Here also William Mayo, John Thornton, Dr. George Nicholas, and other outstanding men took up large tracts in the 1720's. The Jeffersons through several generations migrated up the river, the first Thomas moving from "Mount Malady" to "Osborne" at the falls in 1679, the year in which William Byrd I began the development of this region. The second Thomas Jefferson commenced the acquisition of tracts above the falls in 1705, but he continued to live at "Osborne" until his death in 1731. His son, Peter, son-in-law of Isham Randolph and father of Thomas, the President, inherited these upper lands and at once took up his residence upon them. He was already purchasing tracts farther up the James near the mouth of the Rivanna.

It was not long before the Randolphs, the Carters, and the Pages began acquiring lands along the Rivanna, and Francis Eppes secured a large grant on the near-by Hardware River. But the largest, and one of the earliest, landowners of this region, the present Albemarle County, was Colonel Nicholas Meriwether, who came not up the James but up the South Anna from his home in Hanover County. In 1727 he secured thirteen thousand acres at the foot of Chestnut Ridge, or Southwest Mountain as it was later called. This tract in time was increased to seventeen thousand acres. Meriwether married a daughter of Colonel Francis Thornton; she subsequently became the wife of the great land speculator and explorer, Dr. Thomas Walker, who thus acquired the "Castle Hill" estate. Charles Lewis, a name to be connected with that of Meriwether in the course of time, secured a grant of twelve thousand acres in the same neighborhood in 1732. Thus we find family connections playing quite as important a part in the piedmont section as in the older tidewater.

During the next decade Scotch-Irishmen crossed the Blue Ridge from the Shenandoah Valley and settled in the western part of what is now Albemarle County, but they were never so numerous or so influential as the Virginians who came up the eastern rivers and established the first homes in the piedmont region.

This piedmont country, in the valleys of the James and the Rappahannock, was a part of the first truly American frontier, as the tidewater region was a frontier to Europe. It was this and similar regions that gave us our Daniel Boones and our George Rogers Clarks; but, as we have seen, the pioneers of this section of the piedmont were no long hunters, no explorers on the grand scale. They were substantial men who made their way up the rivers and established for themselves baronial estates upon their banks. Most of the early land grants were generous ones, covering from one to fifteen thousand acres—not large enough for speculating enterprises, except in the case of Spotswood and his associates, but large enough to last any growing family for several generations, with perhaps some left over to sell when a favorable opportunity arose. In some cases tenants were settled on these estates to make the improvements required by law. The owner himself did not always undergo all the hardships of hewing a home out of the wilderness, but migrated to his new seat only after the axe and the plowshare had facilitated the way. There was, it is true, some speculation but not much of the high-pressure type where a quick turnover was expected, and there was not a great deal of absentee ownership. When one had to pay cash for his land, even though the price was low, and, in addition to paying quitrents, cultivate three acres out of every fifty, speculation on an extensive scale was difficult except in cases where the law could be circumvented as Spotswood had done.

Though the first grant within the area of Albemarle County was made in 1727, it was not until 1735 that small tracts were taken up in large numbers; yet there were a few of these scattered among the earlier large ones. This, of course, indicates that the humbler citizen followed his wealthier neighbor into the back country instead of leading the way, as is commonly supposed. But what of the ex-indentured servant, the poor man who goes into the woods to seek a home when he is not able to buy land in the settled areas? It is to be taken for granted that there were some squatters in the piedmont region before the lands were sold, and both Spotswood and William Byrd II state that the back country was in places infested with such people, of whom they both give highly unflattering accounts; but in the actual records of settlement one finds few traces of them in this region. The only possible explanation is that squatters were careful to seek out places where the sheriff and the constable, whose duties included the making out of tithe lists and the collection of quitrents, were not likely to find them. The main rivers hardly afforded such a refuge. Moreover, the planters needed tenants and overseers, and the tithe lists for this period show that there was a substantial number of white men

[47]

thus employed. Peter Jefferson, for instance, employed a steward and five overseers, and he was not so large a landowner as were some of his neighbors. In addition, there were white craftsmen and laborers who worked for wages. All told, there was a considerable number of free whites who were neither landowners nor squatters, and some of them, particularly among the overseers, were quite respectable people, trusted by their employers and able to rise gradually into the more prosperous classes. These facts would seem to explain the relative absence of squatters from the region under discussion, and also go far toward explaining the statement made by various travelers of a later period to the effect that Virginia had very little of the shiftless and degraded population found in other parts of the South.

When we come to the section of the piedmont country which was drained by the Roanoke River and included in the Brunswick County of 1720, we face a rather different situation. Though the land was of average fertility, the Roanoke afforded no good port for the marketing of tobacco and other products, and much of the trade of the region found its way overland to Norfolk. The expense involved in carrying on such a commerce did not encourage the establishment of large plantations which depended upon the outside world for a market. Small self-sustaining farms would be much more likely to prosper; for by this time the poorer people, unlike their seventeenth century prototypes, had adapted themselves to their environment and were able to produce with their own hands practically all the essentials for simple agricultural life. They could spin and weave, make soap and candles, and kill ample game with their long, accurate "Pennsylvania" rifles.

The Roanoke country was to be for a long time a region of small farmers; but, as in the case of the other two river valleys, it was the wealthy landowner who spied out the land and helped himself to some of the best tracts. Yet there was a difference here. The large-scale purchasers were fewer in number, their tracts were more extensive, and they were bought chiefly for speculative purposes. The first to come was William Byrd II, who viewed the land as he was surveying the dividing line between Virginia and North Carolina in 1728. It was in the very year when he was making the survey that he purchased a handsome tract which included Occaneechee Island, on which famous Indian townsite he built a hunting lodge and called it

"Bluestone Castle." Within a few years Byrd was followed by Richard Randolph of "Curles," who explored the area and acquired large tracts, one of which in time passed to his grandson, John of Roanoke. But it was Byrd rather than Randolph who was the great magnate of the region. In 1733, in company with John Banister and William Mayo, he explored the country, naming streams for his companions. In 1742 he eclipsed Spotswood by acquiring a tract of 105,000 acres on the Banister River, a tributary of the Dan; and shortly afterward several large tracts in western Brunswick, or Lunenburg as this area became in 1745, were granted to groups of speculators.

The making of such enormous grants began to be common practice in Virginia about the year 1730, and it grew out of certain peculiar conditions which require some explanation.

Though Brunswick County was created by the Assembly in 1720, we have no record indicating settlement prior to 1722, and the county was not actually organized until 1732. Even then people came in so slowly that in 1738 the Assembly passed an act exempting settlers from taxation for a period of ten years, and permitting all public fees to be paid in tobacco at the high valuation of three pence per pound. A few families had come in before this date. Most of them were from eastern Virginia, but by that year a family of Clouds had arrived from Pennsylvania. They were originally English Quakers, and so far as known were the first immigrants from Pennsylvania to settle in this region. In the same year a Scotch-Presbyterian, one John Caldwell, grandfather to John Caldwell Calhoun, applied to the Synod of Philadelphia, asking that that body send to Governor William Gooch of Virginia and secure his permission for the planting of a colony in that province. Since the passage of the Toleration Act in 1689, it was not necessary for dissenters to get permission merely to settle, but the privilege of public worship could not be enjoyed without official consent. The permit was obtained, and Caldwell led a number of families from Pennsylvania and settled on Cub Creek, a tributary of the Roanoke. Among other Scotch-Irish families settling in the same neighborhood at about this time were the Calhouns, the Calloways, Callighans, and others.

It cannot be stated with certainty whether these Pennsylvania immigrants came down the Great Warrior's Trace through the Valley or whether they followed the route of the Occaneechee Trace from the eastward. Since the lower Valley was not settled as early as 1738, it is more likely that they took the eastern route which passed through settled areas and was somewhat shorter than the other. It was not many years before several Presbyterian congregations were established in eastern Brunswick; and some of the Scotch-Irish, though holding only small plots of land which in most cases they were not able to purchase until several years after their arrival, attained to positions of importance in their communities, such as constable and justice of the peace.

In western Brunswick the situation was somewhat different. It was here that the speculators acquired most of the large grants, and it was here that the Scotch-Irish were most numerous. They did not come into this region much before 1745, when Lunenburg County was created, and they migrated down the Valley over the Great Warrior's Trace. Many of them had tarried in the Valley for a while before moving southward, and many later journeyed on into Tennessee and the Carolinas. For instance, William Bean was living in Augusta County in 1742; in 1746 he was a resident of Lunenburg; and in 1768 he became the first known settler in the Tennessee country. The Renfro and

Walden families, like many others, followed a similar course. In fact, it appears that Brunswick and Lunenburg furnished more of the Tennessee pioneers than did any other section. Of these, John Donelson, originally of Accomac, and Daniel Smith were conspicuous on the Tennessee frontier. Many of the pioneers of western North Carolina and Kentucky also came from this section, notably the Logan, Lane, and Pickens families.

The reason for this is obvious. The main route through the Valley, the oft-mentioned Warrior's Trace, did not continue westward but crossed the Blue Ridge at the Staunton River water gap, or at Maggotty's Gap near by, and passed into Lunenburg and then into the Carolinas. The immigrants followed this obvious route, and it was not until 1768 that settlers reached the Holston River on the Virginia-Tennessee frontier.

When the settler in Lunenburg faced the problem of acquiring a homestead, his situation was essentially different from that of the pioneers of more accessible regions. When the newcomer in Albemarle, for instance, wished to purchase a small tract, the chances were that he had not traveled more than a hundred miles from his former home, and the courthouse at which he would have to arrange for his survey and purchase would not likely be so distant. The expenses of such journeys, as well as surveyor's fees and headrights, might well be defrayed from the proceeds of his former holdings or he might acquire the capital by working as overseer or craftsman. But when a man had migrated from the north of Ireland to Pennsylvania, worked out an indenture there, and then made his way through newly settled country to such an undeveloped region as Lunenburg, the chances were that he did not take with him a very large stock of this world's goods. The records show this to have been true in most cases.

Now many of the large grants made to speculators in the period beginning with the year 1730 were not upon the usual terms of ten shillings the hundred acres, with an annual quitrent of two shillings the hundred and the requirement that three acres in every fifty should be cultivated. Instead, it was provided that the grantees should settle one family upon the land for every thousand acres. A certain number of years was allowed for making these settlements; there was no requirement as to improvements; and quitrents did not have to be paid until patents were issued.

In some cases the grantees brought families direct from Ireland, but if others came of their own volition from Pennsylvania, they were welcomed, for each one was worth a thousand acres to the speculators, who were glad enough to allow the newcomers some time in which to pay for their farms. The speculators usually charged and received three pounds the hundred acres for their lands. This was six times what the public lands sold for, but the stranger in a strange land was willing to pay this sum if he were given time in which to do it, rather than compete for a good location and journey to a distant courthouse to make arrangements with county and colonial officials who might delay his business indefinitely. This situation worked to the advantage of the speculators, and it probably facilitated the settlement of the country.

A similar condition existed in the Valley of Virginia, which term is applied to the territory lying between the Blue Ridge and the Allegheny Mountains, watered in its northern extent by the Shenandoah and in its southern by the New or Kanawha River. The first known settler to establish himself in this country was one Adam Miller, or Müller, a German from Lancaster County, Pennsylvania. According to tradition, he was visiting eastern Virginia when apprised of Spotswood's journey of

1716 to the waters of the Shenandoah. Following in the Governor's footsteps, he crossed the Blue Ridge at Swift Run Gap and selected a tract of land just opposite, on the far side of the mountains. Returning to Lancaster County, he brought a group of families with him and took up his residence near the present town of Elkton in 1726 or 1727. In 1729 Robert Carter and Mann Page marked out a tract of fifty thousand acres on the lower Shenandoah, for which they secured a grant from Lord Fairfax, who claimed the northern end of the Valley as a part of his holdings.

During the same year the Valley was visited by a Pennsylvania German named Jacob Stover, who was apparently working in collaboration with the Van Meter family, Indian traders of New York, New Jersey, and Pennsylvania. In 1730 the Virginia Council made grants of ten thousand acres to Stover and thirty thousand to the Van Meters on condition that they would settle one family for every thousand acres. These were the first of such grants, but numerous others followed. In 1736 William Beverley, grandson of William Byrd I, secured on the same terms more than a hundred thousand acres, including the present site of Staunton. At about the same time, Benjamin Borden, a speculator from New Jersey, obtained an equally extensive tract just southward of Beverley's; and in 1745 James Patton, a Scotch-Irish ship captain who had been employed by Beverley to bring settlers from his native land, secured one hundred thousand acres still farther down the Valley. In 1749 the governor and Council authorized the Loyal Land Company to take up eight hundred thousand acres along the North Carolina border. In this last case there was no requirement either of settlement or improvement; it was necessary only to survey the land, and, as no definite boundaries were fixed, the company might survey any number of tracts within a vast area. Thus the best lands in the Valley were granted to speculators, and the conditions of settlement were similar to those in western Brunswick and Lunenburg counties.

Taking these two areas together, they encircled the older settlements of the tidewater and piedmont regions. They were occupied by diverse national groups, and the conditions under which they were acquired differed from those prevailing in the lands to the eastward. Self-sustaining small farmers predominated here, whereas a type of agriculture dependent upon the tobacco trade prevailed in central piedmont as well as in tidewater.

It is true that the farmers of the central piedmont were farther removed from their markets than were the tidewater inhabitants. They had to boat their crops down the small streams to the head of navigation on the principal rivers, and bring their English manufactures back up the streams in the same way or else haul them overland. The expense involved in this transportation was heavy, but this disadvantage was largely offset by the fact that the piedmont lands were newer and hence more fertile than the depleted fields of tidewater. Nevertheless, the situation encouraged the development of local manufactures in the former section, and even among the large landowners the economy was much more self-sustaining than it was on the seaboard.

As economic conditions differed in the various sections, so did the political and social scene. The aristocratic institutions which prevailed in tidewater were transferred to the piedmont virtually without change, for the people of the latter region came largely from the former, and the economic environment was not sufficiently different to require much readjustment. On the other hand, the Valley and the Southwest were dissimilar both in population and in economic position. The greater democracy of the last-named areas was not due solely to the fact that yeomen farmers predominated, for this element was more numerous than were large landowners in all sections of Virginia. It was due partly to the lack of the aristocratic tradition, and of the aristocrats.

But the western areas were not without their leadership, as is attested by the prominence of such families as the Campbells, the Prestons, the Pattons, the McDowells, the Hites, the Innesses, and the Donelsons. Some of these families, like the Innesses and Donelsons, were from eastern Virginia; some, like the Hites, were Pennsylvania Germans; but most of them were of the Scotch-Irish strain. These last went in more for the Presbyterian ministry, for land speculation and Indian fighting, for politics and public affairs, than for the easy life of the tidewater planter. Their leadership was as powerful in their respective bailiwicks as was that of the old Virginia families east of the mountains. It was marked more by vigorous action than by dignified tradition, and for that reason perhaps it was less stable. But there was a unifying force in that the same law applied in all the regions discussed, and this law was aristocratic in tone. Previous to the Revolution the frontier was never able to set up its own government or to carry out any democratic theories that it might have harbored. But the back country was never prolific of theories; nor, in the period between Bacon's Rebellion and the Revolution, did it ever manifest any desire to set up an establishment of its own. In other words, the law and the necessity for leadership were stronger than democracy even on the frontier and among Scotch-Irishmen; and however much the social scene changed from the aristocratic tradition, it was a long time before this could make itself felt in a political way.

The piedmont and Valley regions thus furnish another illustration of the fact that frontier conditions do not necessarily produce democratic institutions, even when the lands are easily accessible to independent small farmers. They also illustrate the fact that the lines of migration followed by the pioneers as they moved westward were not determined by geographical factors alone. Relative prices of land in various localities were a potent factor, especially in the case of the migration from Pennsylvania, where the Penns charged from ten to fifteen pounds the hundred acres, to Virginia where the public price during the eighteenth century was ten shillings for the same amount. The activities of speculators were able to deflect the course of migration, as in the case of Spotswood when he turned the movement from the James to the valley of the Rappahannock; but in this instance special legislation supplemented the schemes of the speculators. And the presence or absence of hostile Indians was a factor that should not be overlooked.

In most cases the pioneers followed obvious routes of travel, such as river valleys and Indian trails, and often occupied the nearest available lands; but sometimes they traveled long distances to reach especially desirable locations, and sometimes the routes which they chose were by no means the obvious ones. For instance, the migration of Pennsylvanians to southwestern Virginia in the 1730's, long before western Pennsylvania or the southern portion of the Valley of Virginia were settled, could hardly be explained on geographical grounds alone.

The westward movement did not roll forward with an orderly and irresistible force like the waves of the sea. On the contrary, it was as fitful as a mountain stream, now swirling, now eddying, and its course was deflected by many crosscurrents. It is unsafe to generalize too much about it, for a knowledge of numerous special conditions is necessary in order to understand any one of its phases.

III

KENTUCKY

B Y the year 1768 the stream of migration had reached the southern extremity of the Valley of Virginia and pioneers who had moved eastward over the Blue Ridge and settled on the upper waters of the Dan now recrossed the mountains and settled in the Holston Valley, thus laying the foundations of the future state of Tennessee. Some of the long parallel valleys lying westward of the Alleghenies had also been penetrated, but British policy and the Indian menace prevented a movement into the Kentucky country until the very eve of the Revolution. Hence it was forty years after pioneers reached the Valley before any appreciable number of them crossed over the great blue ramparts to the remote region which they called "the land on the Western Waters."

During 1773 Lord Dunmore, governor of Virginia, sent the first surveyors into that country, and futile attempts to establish settlements were made

the next year. In 1775 the first permanent settlements were made almost simultaneously at Har-
rodsburg and Boonesborough. Thus was established a frontier that differed markedly from those
preceding it. Kentucky was not as far removed
from its base of supplies as had been the settlement
at Jamestown, but it was many a weary mile down
the Ohio from Wheeling or Pittsburgh to the
mouth of the Limestone Creek, and then overland
to the Bluegrass region. And it was a still more
arduous journey down the Valley of Virginia to
the Holston Valley, and thence through Cumber-
land Gap and along Boone's Wilderness Trace to
the Crab Orchard in central Kentucky. By the
northern route Scotch-Irishmen from western
Pennsylvania and upcountry Virginians made their
way westward, while the southern route was used
chiefly by homeseekers from the piedmont and Valley regions of Virginia. And so the upcountry Virginia element came to dominate in Kentucky, but
there was a strong and active Pennsylvania contingent.

The fact that the Kentucky pioneers penetrated
so far into the interior and braved an ever-present
Indian menace shows that there was something
more involved than cheap lands and a people seek-

ing an economic escape. The Bluegrass lands were
the best available within the confines of Virginia,
and they were sought by strong and determined
men. Legal claims were fastened upon the choicest
tracts before settlers began to arrive in appreciable
numbers, and most of the newcomers found it necessary to purchase land from the speculators who
had preceded them. Prior to 1800, prices as high
as one hundred dollars per acre were paid in this
region, and even the wealthier planters held no
more than a few hundred acres. Thus it was obvious that the Bluegrass country was never a poor
man's frontier, despite the fact that Daniel Boone
was its first famous citizen.

Yet many drifters did push their way into central
Kentucky, especially after the Indian threat was
largely removed in 1795. Finding all the best lands
taken up, they became river boatmen or tenants, or
settled in the poorer area that surrounded the Bluegrass country. Since the lands south of Green River
had been reserved for Revolutionary veterans of
Virginia who had taken up only a part of the
available acreage, many of the landless emigrants
settled here, and in 1795 they were allowed preemption of two hundred acres at thirty dollars the
hundred. In most cases they found themselves un-

able to pay this price, and the state of Kentucky granted them various extensions.

Thus in two regions, not very widely separated but differing much in the quality of soil, we have two distinct types of frontier settlement. Elsewhere in Kentucky there were sections in which, because of the difference in soil and transportation facilities and also because of the particular circumstances under which the lands were surveyed and settled, one would find every gradation between the wealth of the Bluegrass and the poverty of the "South Country."

As a result of such conditions of settlement, Kentucky came to have a population unlike that of any section of Old Virginia. The real pioneers, such as the Harrods, the McAfees and Calloways, Benjamin Logan, John Floyd, and Daniel Boone, the men who did the actual exploration and surveying, usually settled down to grow up with the country in case the Indians did not put an untimely end to their days. On the other hand, the real leaders of early Kentucky were often the employers of the surveyors and explorers and they, in most cases, migrated to that frontier a few years after the ground had first been broken. Most of them, such as the Browns, the Todds, the Bullitts, the

Breckinridges, the McDowells, the Harts, George Nicholas, Harry Innes, Caleb Wallace, Thomas Marshall, and James Wilkinson, were in the country before 1795.

These barons of the Bluegrass were nearly all from Virginia, but the Presbyterian element of the Valley was far more conspicuous than were the scions of Anglican tidewater. Nor were they at all like the Peter Jeffersons of the piedmont region—substantial planters and magistrates whose main interest, despite various speculative ventures, was in their agricultural operations and who, with little expectation either of profit or pleasure, attended to their offices of vestrymen and justices as a matter of duty.

Most of the Bluegrass leaders were speculators on their own account; and some were lawyers who represented still more important absentee speculators like Robert Morris, the great merchant of Philadelphia, who in 1796 advertised six hundred thousand acres of Kentucky land for sale. In the rank below them there were not enough men of property and stability to fill the commissions of the peace, and in the columns of the *Kentucky Gazette* of Lexington one reads frequent complaints of the shoddy characters who lowered the dignity of the squirearchy. As for the rank and file of the planters and yeomen, there were few who were secure in the titles to their lands, and few who had confidence in their leaders. Furthermore, unlike the inhabitants of the older-settled areas, many lived on lands to which they had no titles at all.

The peculiarities of this frontier were due, therefore, not to simplicity and equality, to free land and opportunity, but to a marked stratification in which no stratum was securely established. Each group was striving for advancement and each was suspicious of the other. But rugged individualism, that famous frontier development which has been so widely advertised by the modern masters of capital, was there in large measure. The early population of Kentucky was restless and aggressive, assertive and self-confident. But if by individualism we mean intellectual independence, we do not find it conspicuous on the frontier. We find, on the contrary, that no man must differ too much from his neighbor in any obvious way. There are few countries in which outward conformity to prevailing standards is so much insisted on as in the United States, and it is the gift of the West to the nation.

For the present purpose our main interest in early Kentucky is due to the fact that it was the first Virginia frontier which had the opportunity to shape its own political institutions. The parent state had that opportunity in 1776, but, as a whole, she was then no longer a frontier community and her work is commonly looked on as a monument to eastern conservatism. It is true that, before she finished, she abolished primogeniture and entails, established religious freedom, reformed her criminal code, and adopted the principle that government derives its powers from the people and that all freemen should be equal in the eyes of the law. But her constitution restricted the suffrage to property holders, as in colonial times, and failed to apportion representation according to population. It also left local government in the hands of appointive officials, the justices of the peace still holding office for life. It remained for the frontier to attack these citadels of conservatism.

After eight years of struggle the Kentucky district achieved her separation from Virginia and in 1792 entered the Union as the fifteenth state. As soon as this event was assured, the problem of drafting a constitution for the new commonwealth occupied the attention of the people; and as early as 1791 an active controversy was under way. Two antagonistic schools of thought presently emerged.

One of these, supported mainly by the slaveholding planters, preferred to hold fast to the institutions of the Old Dominion, with a property qualification for voters, a legislature made up of two chambers, and a bill of rights. The other school advocated manhood suffrage and the division of the counties into precincts where the voting should be by ballot instead of at the county seat by the old viva-voce method. It also stood for representation apportioned among the counties according to population, a one-chambered legislature, popular election of all local and most state officials, and, strangely enough, for abolishing the bill of rights. Although these were not constitutional questions, the radicals wished also to provide for the payment of taxes in kind and manifested a strong antipathy toward lawyers, desiring, partly as a means of dispensing with their services, to prohibit the use of British legal precedents in judicial proceedings and to adopt a simplified system of law.

In seeking for the origin of the ideas of this group, one finds many of them in the Pennsylvania constitution of 1776—the most radical of such Revolutionary documents, which the Pennsylvanians themselves had already discarded in 1790. Here are found the unicameral legislature and the

vote by ballot which the radical Kentuckians desired. But here is also to be found a provision that
officeholders must believe in the inspiration of the
Scriptures. A similar provision was contained in
the first constitutions of North Carolina and Tennessee, but not in that of Virginia; nor did the
Kentuckians propose it. They did propose, however, to exclude "immoral" men from office. Thus
the naïveté of the Presbyterian influence among the
radicals is disclosed. It is interesting to know that
Tom Paine's *Rights of Man* was often quoted with
approval by the same group.

The most extraordinary proposal of the Kentucky radicals was that which called for dispensing
with a bill of rights, a feature which the first Pennsylvania constitution had not omitted. This is explained by the fact that the gradual abolition of
slavery was one of the chief aims of the radicals,
and since the bill of rights carried a guarantee of
property, this might prove an obstacle in their
path.

The changes desired in the method of voting
were intended to get rid of the Virginia system
under which the county magnates, by dispensing
drinks at the courthouse on election day and keep-
ing an eye on the progress of the voting, could eas-

ily entice the freeholders into camp. It was alleged that under the old regime in Kentucky, the candidate, "with a low bow and a 'thank you, sir,'" would express his appreciation to each voter for his support. The commonalty here apparently had developed a strong dislike not only of lawyers but of colonels and squires and laced cuffs and powdered wigs. They wished to get "aristocrats" out of office and put honest farmers in their places, whereas the more privileged elements did not hesitate to say that the farmers were too ignorant to be entrusted with the conduct of public business. Thus we have evidence of overt class antagonism in Kentucky which had not come to the surface on any earlier frontier of Virginia, and which was not inevitably a product of frontier life. Agriculture did not ordinarily bring classes into conflict even where slavery existed, but land speculation and insecure land titles did. Naturally, the mingling of Pennsylvania with Virginia elements in the population also played a part in the controversy.

Hence, though the situation in Kentucky differed from that which was typical of earlier frontiers, it was a scene which, with variations in every case, occurred over and over again in the development of the later American West. The frontier democracy which it evolved was, therefore, of more than local significance. Consequently, it is well to note that a part of it came from the Philadelphia constitutional convention of 1776, which, while not dominated by the conservative "east," was hardly a frontier gathering. In fact, it would be difficult to show that our western frontiers have ever produced anything much more radically democratic than did the Philadelphia convention in the year of our independence.

On the other hand, there was an element of Kentucky radicalism which did not come from Philadelphia and which really bares the heart of frontier democracy. The desire to dispense with a bill of rights reveals this factor. The leaders of the American Revolution were trained in the school of colonial politics and well read in the philosophy of the eighteenth century. Throughout the latter part of the colonial period they had struggled stubbornly for local self-government and for the right of all freemen to equality before the law, which involved such juridical privileges as trial by jury, and exemption from arbitrary arrest and from unwarranted searches and seizures. In spite of Jefferson's "glittering generality," they did not believe in human equality; but they did believe that a majority might be just as tyrannical as a king, and that the fundamental rights of the individual should for all time be safeguarded against the action of any government whatsoever. This was the object of the bill of rights.

Now when the Kentucky radicals proposed to dispense with such guarantees, they thought that they were doing it in the interest of human freedom, but actually they were striking at the roots of freedom and proposing to subject all men to the mere will of the majority. And this is the keynote of frontier democracy. It cared little for principles or for the rights of the individual. It wished to carry its point, whatever that point might happen to be at any given moment, by popular action; it cared for numbers more than it did for leadership; it despised the superior man—unless he happened to be useful for the time being—just because he was superior; and it strove to put the bottom rail on top, whereas an enlightened government would attempt, as Jefferson wished, to raise the bottom rail toward the top.

The bottom rail had an unusually good opportunity to assert itself in central Kentucky, for the unbroken country permitted fairly thick settlement, and, unlike tidewater Virginia, trade and manu-

facture developed a number of small towns. Moreover, the editor of Kentucky's oldest newspaper,
John Bradford of the *Gazette,* was sympathetic to
the popular cause and gave it wide publicity. Young
Henry Clay, a newcomer to the state, also supported the cause, as did General John Adair and
Felix Grundy, its chief sachem. But Grundy did not
come to the fore until somewhat after this period,
and Clay had not yet made a name for himself.
Most of the recognized leaders in Kentucky, men
who had established their reputations when Virginia still held sway, were on the other side. The
two most powerful of these were George Nicholas
and John Breckinridge, and none was able effec-
tively to challenge them.

The viva-voce method of voting was still in
effect and this worked in favor of the established
leaders. In order to overcome this handicap, the
radicals began their constitutional campaign in
1791 by organizing county committees. It is not
certain whether they got the idea from the county
committees of Revolutionary times or from the
western Pennsylvanians who in the same year organized such bodies to protest against the new Federal excise tax, for they cited both precedents for
their action.

Under the Virginia system, counties were divided into military districts in each of which a militia company was organized. Every district was now requested to elect two delegates to a county committee. Before the constitutional controversy was over, most of the counties took some action but there was no great enthusiasm; and the Bourbon committee, under the leadership of an obscure person by the name of William Henry, was the only one that functioned with any vigor.

The plan was to have the county committees nominate delegates to the convention and draw up instructions for their guidance. In this way it was hoped to defeat the lawyers and aristocrats and put affairs into the hands of the simple farmers. But when the elections took place, the radical candidates were usually defeated and the conservatives, under the leadership of George Nicholas, were firmly in control.

Yet the constitution which was drafted by the convention of 1792 has often been pointed out as a triumph of frontier democracy, for it was the first in the nation to grant manhood suffrage. This, however, was hardly such a radical step as it might seem, for land claims in Kentucky overlapped each other like shingles on a roof and titles were so subject to controversy that it would have been impossible to determine who were the freeholders. The eight previous conventions which had assembled in Kentucky to discuss the question of separation from Virginia had been elected on a manhood suffrage basis, and this was certainly the most practicable arrangement in the circumstances, though up to this time Virginia law still required the freehold qualification in regular elections.

Not only was manhood suffrage provided by the constitution of 1792, but the ballot was substituted for the old viva-voce method of voting. This was intended to undermine the power of the county magnates, with their pernicious rum and their handshaking on election day. It would thus appear that the radicals had won much. In reality their victory was a hollow one, for the governor and the Senate were to be chosen by an electoral college, and judges and justices of the peace, as well as most other officials, were to be appointed by the governor. This entrenched the upper class in all branches of government, and the conservatives had nothing to fear. They had made important concessions to the masses but at the same time had safeguarded their own position. They kept their bill of rights and upheld the institution of slavery by an overwhelming vote, only Harry Innes and the eleven clergymen who were members of the convention voting against article eleven, which secured it. All this was truly typical of frontier politics. The making of apparent concessions to the masses while entrenching and safeguarding essential interests was the usual policy adopted by the conservative minority, and it was always aided by lethargy and lack of information on the part of the rank and file.

No sooner was the constitution adopted than the radicals raised their voices against it. Their leaders and their arguments were much the same as they had been before the convention assembled, and their complaints were directed particularly against the choice of governor and Senate by an electoral college and against perpetuation of slavery. They demanded immediate provision for another convention and in 1794 the House passed a bill calling for a new election on the subject, but the Senate defeated the move and the agitation continued.

The victory of the conservatives in the matter of the constitution did not mean that Kentucky was to make no political progress during the next few years. Her population was growing rapidly, thanks to the defeat of the northern Indians at the battle of Fallen Timbers in 1794 and to the opening of the Mississippi River to American commerce by Pinckney's Treaty in 1795. Settlers to the number of 2,460 came in over the Wilderness Trace during the first five months of this year, and the legislature made provision for opening a wagon road along the route. Pack horses were giving place to wheeled vehicles in the overland trade; Kentucky horses and cattle were being driven to eastern markets in ever-increasing numbers; and tobacco, flour, and salt meat were being shipped down the Ohio and Mississippi to the New Orleans market. Whiskey was even then an important Kentucky product, but, unlike the Pennsylvanians, these Westerners did not resort to violence in opposing the Federal excise tax, though there was some resentment against it.

Questions concerning lands, both public and private, were never out of the minds of Kentuckians during these years, and the action of the government regarding them furnishes one of the best indexes of its relative liberality or conservatism. Most of the early Virginia claims had been adjudicated by a commission appointed in 1779 for that purpose, and until 1794 its findings had always been considered as final. In that year Kentucky's Supreme Court of Appeals decided, in the case of

[79]

Kenton *v.* McConnell, that the rulings of this early commission were subject to judicial review, thereby calling into question the titles to more than a million acres of the best lands in the state. Judges George Muter and Benjamin Sebastian of the higher tribunal were already under suspicion for complicity in the notorious "Spanish Conspiracy," and it was widely believed that George Nicholas, attorney for McConnell, had influenced this decision. Attempts were made to have the judges impeached or removed from office by the legislature, for that body had such authority, but nothing was done in this direction although a futile reprimand was illegally adopted by a bare majority. The pressure of public opinion was strong, however, and during the next year Judge Muter yielded to it, docilely changed his opinion, and quieted the storm. The original holders of the lands in question were largely Virginians and early Kentucky pioneers. Most of them had sold to the wealthier settlers and guaranteed the titles; consequently an important, though not a powerful, group of people would have been ruined by the controversial decision. The fact that the interests of speculators, largely absentees, seemed to outweigh the interests of the actual pioneers and settlers, not only with the highest Kentucky court but with the legislature as well, does not speak favorably for political conditions in the state. Indeed, it cannot be denied that most of Kentucky's early leaders showed themselves subject, in varying degree, to sinister influences in connection with the Spanish Conspiracy, but such influences scarcely reached the rank and file and a surprising amount of really progressive legislation was passed during this period.

It was in 1795 that the settlers south of Green River were allowed to preëmpt two hundred acres including their improvements; the principle of preemption was again applied fifteen years later when the "Tellico" lands were opened to settlement. In 1800 Kentucky became so anxious for settlers that she offered to sell four hundred acres at twenty dollars the hundred to any male citizen of the United States or to any foreigner who would take an oath of allegiance, provided only that he would settle upon the land. In 1809 it was enacted that any claimant who had occupied his tract for seven years should not thereafter be disturbed by adverse claims; and in 1811 a law was passed which stipulated that any occupying claimant who had to give up his settlement should be paid for all improvements which he had made upon the land, though he was not required to pay rent for the period of his occupancy.

Taken as a whole, this body of legislation was highly favorable to the settler as against the speculator and goes far toward showing that the circumstances surrounding the decision of Muter and Sebastian in the case of Kenton *v.* McConnell were of a temporary nature rather than of permanent significance. The legislature even under a conservative regime was, after all, reasonably responsive to the economic interests of the masses. Intellectual interests were altogether another matter. Though Transylvania Seminary had been established in 1783, the Kentucky constitution of 1792 made no provision for public education, whereas this had been done by both Georgia and North Carolina.

Yet really encouraging signs of enlightenment were not lacking. The constitution abolished imprisonment for debt except in cases where fraud was suspected, provided the debtor surrendered his property to his creditors. In 1796 entail was abolished, and in 1798 the penal code was revised according to the best contemporary practice. The death penalty was retained only in the case of first degree murder, benefit of clergy was abolished, and a penitentiary was established. This was indeed notable progress for a frontier state.

The question of reforming the constitution itself was not dead. From 1793 onward the issue bobbed up from time to time, and the reformers gradually centered their attention more and more upon the two principal issues: dispensing with the electoral college for the choice of governor and Senate, and the abolition of slavery. Committees on the old plan were formed in a number of counties, William Henry of Bourbon again taking the lead, but complaints were made that committee business was sometimes carried on without sufficient public notice. In some cases the conservatives organized committees of their own, and George Nicholas took a prominent part in the proceedings of one which convened at Bryan's Station. Here he came out strongly against the abolition of slavery, saying that he had inherited the slaves belonging to him and that he had never bought or sold a Negro except where it was necessary for disciplinary purposes or in order to prevent the separation of families. He charged that the abolitionists were unwilling to bear any part of the economic loss that emancipation would entail, and maintained that

[83]

the Negroes were too lazy, too ignorant, and too undisciplined to shift for themselves as freemen. He also pointed out that any person who wished to free his own slaves was at liberty to do so.

It is a striking fact that Nicholas, while thus taking the lead in supporting the cause of the conservatives in Kentucky, was at the same time, together with Breckinridge, collaborating with the Sage of Monticello in securing adoption by the Kentucky legislature of Jefferson's famous resolutions of 1798. Indeed, no group of men in the country was more conspicuous in the councils of Jeffersonian Republicanism than were these Kentucky conservatives. The opposition to Hamilton's financial measures, to Federalistic nationalism, and to the rule of the "wealthy and well born," had developed in Kentucky as early as anywhere in the nation; and this youngest of the states was a leader rather than a follower in the Republican cause.

These facts reveal the essence of early Jeffersonian Republicanism. It did not stand for any leveling principles, but maintained the old Revolutionary doctrine of equality before the law; and it desired to make that law more liberal and just, as is plainly shown by the reform of the criminal code and the establishment of a penitentiary in Kentucky in this same year. But the very men who were being called aristocrats in Kentucky were themselves denouncing the Federalists as aristocrats. To the Republican mind, an aristocrat was a man who gained his wealth in some way other than from the products of the soil and of human labor. The mechanic as well as the farmer and the slaveholding planter was entitled to what he gained; but, as the Republicans saw it, commercial and financial operations brought unearned profits and those who received them were aristocrats, sometimes referred to as "paper aristocrats." In other words, early Jeffersonian Republicanism was a liberal agrarian aristocracy pitted against an acquisitive bourgeois oligarchy, and sectionalism was, of course, involved in the struggle.

Nicholas and Breckinridge with their following gained much credit in Kentucky as a result of their participation in the struggle over the Alien and Sedition Acts. Such a reaction was genuine, for not only had the Federalists made themselves unpopular in Kentucky by their western policy, but their Alien and Sedition Acts infringed the fundamental principle of equality before the law.

Thus the radicals were going up against strong opposition in their fight on the constitutional question. The document of 1792 had provided that in the general election of 1797 the people should vote on the matter of calling a new convention and if a majority should approve such a call, then the legislature should authorize a similar poll to be taken the next year; if a majority of voters again approved, a convention would be assembled to amend or revise the constitution. But if, at either election, a majority did not favor the convention, then the legislature was authorized to call one by a two-thirds vote.

The unpopularly elected Senate had blocked previous moves to call a convention, but the vote was taken in 1797 as provided by the constitution; and since a majority of those voting for representatives did not vote for the convention, no ballot on the question was authorized for the following year. Nevertheless, the committees advised that the citizens vote on their own initiative, and there was this time a larger affirmative ballot than previously; but there was still not a clear majority. However, the legislature proceeded to authorize the election of a convention to meet the next year. In both elections the Bluegrass showed the least enthusiasm for a convention, most of the support coming from the poorer counties surrounding it. Since the radi-

cal committees had not been able to get out a sufficient vote to compel the calling of the convention,
it appears that popular interest in their cause was
lukewarm and that the established leaders of the
legislature went rather far in the direction of liberalism when they called the convention of their own
accord. They were evidently not greatly disturbed
as to the issue.

Both conservative and radical committees nom-
inated tickets in Fayette County, whose seat of
justice, Lexington, was the metropolis of the Bluegrass region. Other committees took similar action,
but the conservatives won a sweeping victory. The
convention which assembled in 1799 abolished the
electoral college and provided for popular election
of both governor and Senate, it is true. But the ap-
pointment of judges, justices of the peace, and most
other officials was still vested in the chief executive;
and there was now only one vote against article
eleven, which secured the institution of slavery.
Not only this, but two important reactionary steps
were taken. The old viva-voce method of voting
was restored, and the constitution was made so difficult to amend that it would be a long time before
slave property would again be threatened. Thus
seven years of agitation brought only such conces-

[87]

sions as the entrenched leaders were willing to make—a consummation which shows clearly that the farmers and laborers of Kentucky were either not seriously inclined to break with tradition or else they lacked the leadership which might have made this possible.

That a different result might have been achieved under different circumstances is demonstrated by an event occurring in 1802. By this time the area south of Green River had been settled by people who mostly still owed the state for their lands, and they were not inclined to be too friendly toward the prosperous Bluegrass section. The "South Country" had the sympathy of the poorer element in other outlying counties, and these people had found a leader in Felix Grundy. He was no innovator from Pennsylvania, but a Virginian and a demagogue who was generously endowed by nature with those gifts which insure a politician's fortune.

The constitution of 1792 had given the Supreme Court original jurisdiction in cases arising under the land laws of Virginia. This was looked upon as an advantage to the wealthier people and to the speculators who did not wish to entrust their interests to the mercies of the unlearned and probably prejudiced justices of the courts of quarter sessions. But the Supreme Court proved inadequate to the business, and a series of district courts was organized and given jurisdiction in land suits. This was convenient enough for men of substance, but the poor farmer would, in many cases, still have to leave his home county and appear before strangers in order to defend his holdings. Therefore, in 1801 Felix Grundy introduced a measure proposing to abolish both the district and the quarter session courts and to combine their jurisdictions in circuit courts to be presided over in each county by one judge and two assistants, it being specifically provided that the latter should be devoid of legal training.

Grundy failed to carry his bill at this time, but he succeeded the next year. Thus the courts were made easily available to the farmers, but the majority of the judges were ignorant men and as a result the administration of justice was cheapened and weakened. Contributing to this outcome were earlier statutes which made the salaries of judges and other officials so low that properly qualified men were not encouraged to enter the public service. On the other hand, justices of the peace, who in Virginia and Kentucky had formerly served without remuneration, were granted fees by an act of 1793. This did not increase their popularity, but, curiously enough, the tenure of the judiciary was not seriously attacked and under both constitutions judges and justices continued to be appointed by the governor, to serve during good behavior.

These may appear to be matters of no great import, but in the colonial period officeholding was usually an honorary, and therefore honorable, position. Leadership was respected, and therefore generally respectable. The breaking down of the ancient position of the justices of the peace was a part of the general trend to substitute a cheap professionalism for dignified amateurism in politics and thereby to introduce one of the worst tendencies into American public life. It was a movement in the direction of democracy, however, for only a man in comfortable circumstances could afford to devote his time, free of charge, to the public service. The change was due partly to the weakness in new country of that stable and prosperous class which had constituted the earlier squirearchy. The vulgarization of the judiciary and of officeholding in general was one of the chief accomplishments of that frontier leveling spirit of which so much has been said by the historians of the West.

Thus we see that the Kentucky radicals, working through popular committees, had accomplished almost nothing, whereas a gifted and ambitious leader, presenting a program designed to catch the fancy of the masses, was able to wield great power. Fortunately such leaders do not appear in every generation, and they have not confined their activities to the frontier; but the fluid conditions existing in new country gave them a rare opportunity. From the days of the Gracchi to modern times, their methods have not greatly changed.

Perhaps the best purpose served by frontier democracy was the pressure which it brought to bear upon the more conservative leaders who, while wishing to protect their interests, were in this period still indoctrinated with the philosophical ideas of the Revolutionary era. It was they and not the radicals who ineffectually brought up the question of public education; and, while not taking the lead in the movement, they put up no real opposition to the granting of manhood suffrage and the apportionment of representation according to population. The really progressive legislation of the period, such as the reform of the penal code, the establishment of the penitentiary, and the abolition of entails, was no part of the program of the radical committees. No popular demand was made along these lines, whereas the one outstanding triumph of the popular party—the establishment of the circuit court system—was a step in the wrong direction.

As far as the first ten years of Kentucky's statehood are concerned, it is safe to say that the popular cause was ineffectual except when led by a talented demagogue, and that its actual accomplishments were undesirable from the point of view of the public interest. On the other hand, the legislation passed by the established leaders was, on the whole, enlightened; and yet, except in the matter of manhood suffrage and representation according to population, it was not more enlightened than the contemporary legislation of Virginia. If we take the circuit court system into account, it would seem that Virginia had the advantage so far as the law was concerned, and she assuredly had a decided advantage in the matter of the administration of the law.

Looking back over the migration of population in Virginia from the Atlantic seaboard to the regions of central Kentucky, certain facts stand out with a fair degree of clarity. The primitive condition of frontier life was one of the factors that

shaped society in its westward march, but it was a
temporary influence and it was not always the para-
mount one. People clung to the customs and traditions which they brought with them to the new
country, and the long arm of the law did not often
permit them to be complete masters of their own
destiny. Moreover, land was never entirely free,
and the actual price set upon it by colony and state
was small in comparison to the time and expense
involved in getting a patent.

The frontier did not advance at an even pace.
Sometimes it moved gradually up the valleys of the
most accessible streams, as in the case of the valley
of the James and its tributaries; but sometimes it
took a much less obvious course, as in the case of
the movement up the Rappahannock and that of
the migration of Pennsylvanians to Southside Virginia. In these instances special legislation, relative
prices and availability of lands, and the operations
of speculators were the factors that somewhat
modified the normal influence of geographical conditions.

In cases where lands were particularly desirable,
as in the Bluegrass region of Kentucky, men moved
long distances from their former homes and faced
incredible hardships in order to acquire them; and

here, as in the case of the tidewater pioneers, considerable capital and industry were necessary to
establish one's self in the distant land. Those who
were able to do so became the leaders in the new
country. In the case of tidewater, most of the other
emigrants had to be transported, in effect, on bor-
rowed capital; and in order to pay the debt the
transportee had to surrender his freedom for a
limited time. Thus a powerful upper class and a
numerous lower class were developed, with the
middle class of yeomen relatively weak during the
early period. When the movement into the piedmont started, land was cheap and distances not so
great, and many yeomen were able to establish
themselves. Consequently, though the aristocratic
regime was maintained under an aristocratic government, the democratic element was always
strong but conservative.

In the settlement of Kentucky the poorer emigrants were able to furnish their own transportation thither, but the best lands had been preëmpted
by speculators and purchasers who could pay the
high prices which were demanded. Therefore, during the early years there was an unusually large
landless element, and the relations existing between
this group and the land-speculator-politicians, who

were the leaders, were not particularly cordial. Since most of the men who had come so far to seek their fortunes were restless and aggressive, much rivalry and jealousy existed between different groups. These conditions are a far cry from the idealized picture of the frontier where simplicity and equalitarianism reign on the verge of the forest, but they are fairly typical of the early Southwest; and it was such a conflict of interests that gave rise to frontier democracy as it existed in that section.

In the circumstances, it is surprising that the entrenched interests were able to control the situation as thoroughly as they did. This was due partly to the fact that both leaders and commonalty were largely from Virginia and therefore devotees of the same governmental ideas. Another factor making for accord was the indoctrination of the leaders, speculators and politicians though they were, with the liberal ideas of the Revolutionary period. Their legislative program was actually more constructive than was that of their democratic rivals.

It should be noted in this connection that democracy is not necessarily the same thing as liberalism. During the early years of statehood in Kentucky, it was really the reverse. The democratic element wished to permit constituents to instruct their representatives on all matters of legislation, to abrogate the bill of rights, and to put the government in the hands of a series of extralegal committees which would have great power but no responsibility. The unobstructed rule of the majority was its aim. This would have been totalitarian government, and we may be thankful that frontier democracy was never to win a decisive victory over the principles of the Revolutionary period as adopted and supported by the Jeffersonian Republicans.